Research Navigator.com Guide: Sociology

Joseph E. Jacoby
Bowling Green State University

Linda R. Barr
University of the Virgin Islands

PEARSON

and

Boston | New York | San Francisco
Mexico City | Montreal | Toronto | London | Madrid | Munich | Paris
Hong Kong | Singapore | Tokyo | Cape Town | Sydney

ISBN   0-205-51724-2

Printed in the United States of America

10 9 8 7 6 5 4 3 2   11 10 09 08 07 06

Contents

Introduction

Your professor assigns a ten-page research paper that's due in two weeks—and you need to make sure you have up-to-date, credible information. Where do you begin? Today, the easiest answer is the Internet—because it can be so convenient and there is so much information out there. But therein lies part of the problem. How do you know if the information is reliable and from a trustworthy source?

ResearchNavigator.com Guide is designed to help you select and evaluate research from the Web to help you find the best and most credible information you can. Throughout this guide, you'll find:

- **A practical and to-the-point discussion of search engines.** Find out which search engines are likely to get you the information you want and how to phrase your searches for the most effective results.
- **Detailed information on evaluating online sources.** Locate credible information on the Web and get tips for thinking critically about Web sites.
- **Citation guidelines for Web resources.** Learn the proper citation guidelines for Web sites, email messages, listservs, and more.
- **ResearchNavigator.com Guide.** All you need to know to get started with ResearchNavigator.com, a research database that gives you immediate access to hundreds of scholarly journals and other popular publications, such as *Scientific American, U.S. News & World Report,* and many others.

So before running straight to your browser, take the time to read through this copy of *ResearchNavigator.com Guide* and use it as a reference for all of your Web research needs.

P A R T 1

Research
Navigator.com

What Is ResearchNavigator.com?

ResearchNavigator.com is the easiest way for you to start a research assignment or research paper. Complete with extensive help on the research process and four exclusive databases of credible and reliable source material (including EBSCO's ContentSelect™ Academic Journal and Abstract Database, *New York Times* Search by Subject Archive, Link Library, and the *Financial Times* Article Archive), ResearchNavigator.com helps you quickly and efficiently make the most of your research time.

ResearchNavigator.com includes four databases of dependable source material to get your research process started:

1. EBSCO's ContentSelect™ Academic Journal and Abstract Database, organized by subject, contains 50–100 of the leading academic journals per discipline. Instructors and students can search the online journals by keyword, topic, or multiple topics. Articles include abstract and citation information and can be cut, pasted, emailed, or saved for later use.

2. The *New York Times* Search by Subject Archive is organized by academic subject and searchable by keyword, or multiple keywords. Instructors and students can view full-text articles from the world's leading journalists from *The New York Times*. The *New York Times* Search by Subject Archive is available exclusively to instructors and students through ResearchNavigator.com.

3. Link Library, organized by subject, offers editorially selected "Best of the Web" sites. Link libraries are continually scanned and kept up to date, providing the most relevant and accurate links for research assignments.

4. The *Financial Times* Article Archive and Company Financials provides a searchable one-year archive and five-year financials for the 500 largest U.S. companies (by gross revenue).

In addition, ResearchNavigator.com includes extensive online content detailing the steps in the research process including:

- Understanding the Research Process
- Finding Sources for your Assignment
- Using your Library for Research, with library guides to 31 core disciplines. Each library guide includes an overview of major databases and online journals, key associations and newsgroups, and suggestions for further research.
- Writing Your Research Assignment
- Finishing with Endnotes and a Bibliography

Registering with ResearchNavigator.com

`http://www.researchnavigator.com`

ResearchNavigator.com is simple to use and easy to navigate. The goal of ResearchNavigator.com is to help you complete research assignments or research papers quickly and efficiently. The site is organized around the following five tabs:

- The Research Process
- Finding Sources
- Using Your Library
- Start Writing
- Endnotes & Bibliography

In order to begin using ResearchNavigator.com, you must first register using the personal access code that appears in the front cover of this book.

To Register:

4. Go to http://www.researchnavigator.com
5. Click "Register" under "New Users" on the left side of the screen.
6. Enter the access code exactly as it appears on the inside front cover of this book. (Note: Access codes can only be used once to com-

plete one registration. If you purchased a used guide, the access code may not work. Please go to **www.researchnavigator.com** for information on how to obtain a new access code.)

7. Follow the instructions on screen to complete your registration—you may click the Help button at any time if you are unsure how to respond.

8. Once you have successfully completed registration, write down the Login Name and Password you just created and keep it in a safe place. You will need to enter it each time you want to revisit ResearchNavigator.com.

9. Once you register, you have access to all the resources in ResearchNavigator.com for twelve months.

Getting Started

From the ResearchNavigator.com homepage, you have easy access to all of the site's main features, including a quick route to four exclusive databases of source content that will be discussed in greater detail on the following pages. If you are new to the research process, you may want to start by clicking the *Research Process* tab, located in the upper right hand section of the page. Here you will find extensive help on all aspects of the research process, including:

- Overview of the Research Process
- Understanding a Research Assignment
- Finding a Topic
- Creating Effective Notes
- Research Paper Paradigms
- Understanding and Finding "Source" Material
- Understanding and Avoiding Plagiarism
- Summary of the Research Process

For those of you who are already familiar with the research process, you already know that the first step in completing a research assignment or research paper is to select a topic. (In some cases, your instructor may assign you a topic.) According to James D. Lester in *Writing Research Papers,* choosing a topic for the research paper can be easy (any topic will serve) yet very complicated (an informed choice is critical). He suggests selecting a person, a person's work, or a specific issue to study—President George W. Bush, John Steinbeck's *Of Mice and Men,* or learned dexterity with Nintendo games. Try to select a topic that will meet three demands.

1. It must examine a significant issue.
2. It must address a knowledgeable reader and carry that reader to another level of knowledge.

3. It must have a serious purpose, one that demands analysis of the issues, argues from a position, and explains complex details.

You can find more tips from Lester in the *Research Process* section of ResearchNavigator.com.

ResearchNavigator.com simplifies your research efforts by giving you a convenient launching pad for gathering data on your topic. The site has aggregated four distinct types of source material commonly used in research assignments: academic journals (Content-Select™); newspaper articles (*New York Times*), World Wide Web sites (Link Library), and international news and business data (*Financial Times*).

EBSCO's ContentSelect Academic Journal and Abstract Database

EBSCO's ContentSelect Academic Journal and Abstract Database contains scholarly, peer-reviewed journals (like the *Journal of Clinical Psychology* or the *Journal of Anthropology*). A scholarly journal is an edited collection of articles written by various authors and is published several times per year. All the issues published in one calendar year comprise a volume of that journal. For example, the *American Sociological Review* published volume 65 in the year 2000. This official journal of the American Sociological Association is published six times a year, so issues 1–6 in volume 65 are the individual issues for that year. Each issue contains between 4 and 8 articles written by a variety of authors. Additionally, journal issues may contain letters from the editor, book reviews, and comments from authors. Each issue of a journal does not necessarily revolve around a common theme. In fact, most issues contain articles on many different topics.

Scholarly journals, are similar to magazines in that they are published several times per year and contain a variety of articles in each issue, however, they are NOT magazines. What sets them apart from popular magazines like *Newsweek* or *Science News* is that the content of each issue is peer-reviewed. This means that each journal has, in addition to an editor and editorial staff, a pool of reviewers. Rather than a staff of writers who write something on assignment, journals accept submissions from academic researchers all over the world. The editor relies on these peer reviewers both to evaluate the articles, which are submitted, and to decide if they should be accepted for publication. These published articles provide you with a specialized knowledge and information about your research topic. Academic journal articles adhere to strict scientific guidelines for methodology and theoretical grounding. The information obtained in these individual articles is more scientific than information you would find in a popular magazine, newspaper article, or on a Web page.

Using ContentSelect

Searching for articles in ContentSelect is easy! Here are some instructions and search tips to help you find articles for your research paper.

Select a Database

ContentSelect's homepage features a list of databases. To search within a single database, click the name of the database. To search in more than one database, hold down the alt or command key while clicking on the name of the database.

Basic Search. After selecting one or more databases, you must enter a keyword or keywords, then click on "go." This will take you to the basic search window. If you've selected a precise and distinctive keyword, your search may be done. But if you have too many results—which is often the case—you need to narrow your search.

Standard Search (Boolean).

- **AND** combines search terms so that each result contains all of the terms. For example, search **education AND technology** to find only articles that contain both terms.
- **OR** combines search terms so that each result contains at least one of the terms. For example, search **education OR technology** to find results that contain either term.
- **NOT** excludes terms so that each result does not contain the term that follows the "not" operator. For example, search **education NOT technology** to find results that contain the term education but not the term technology.

Search by Article Number. Each and every article in the EBSCO ContentSelect Academic Journal and Abstract Database is assigned its own unique article number. In some cases, you may know the exact article number for the journal article you'd like to retrieve. Perhaps you noted it during a prior research session on ResearchNavigator.com. Such article numbers might also be found on a companion web site for your text, or in the text itself.

To retrieve a specific article, simply type that article number in the "Search by Article Number" field and click the **GO** button.

Advanced Search.   On the tabbed tool bar, click **Advanced Search.** The advanced search window appears. Enter your search terms in the **Find** field. Your search terms can be keywords or selections from search history. Boolean operators (AND, OR, NOT) can also be included in your search.

You can also use **field codes** with your search terms. Fields refer to searchable aspects of an article or Web page; in the case of ContentSelect, they include author, title, subject, abstract, and journal name. Click **Field Codes** to display a list of field codes available with the databases you are using. Type the field code before your search terms to limit those words to the field you entered. For example, **AU Naughton** will find records that contain Naughton in the author field.

To **print, e-mail, or save** several search results, click on the folder next to the result; then print, e-mail, or save from the folder at the top of the results field. (You can still print, e-mail, or save individual results from the open article or citation.)

You can remove specific results, or clear the entire folder and collect new results, during your session. If you end your session, or it times out due to inactivity, the folder is automatically cleared.

Full-Text Results.   Some ContentSelect results will be available in full text—that is, if you click on the full text logo at the bottom of an entry, you will be able to call up the entire journal or magazine article. If you want to limit your search to results available in full text, click on the "search options" tab, and then on "full text." Then renew your search.

Abstract and Citation Results.   Many ContentSelect results are in the form of citations containing abstracts. A **citation** is a bibliographic reference to an article or document, with basic information such as ISSN (International Standard Serial Number, the standard method for identifying publications) and publisher that will help you locate it. An **abstract** is a brief description of an article, usually written by the author. An abstract will help you decide whether you want to locate the work—either in an electronic database or a print version—through your college library.

A handy tip: once you have found an article that meets your research needs, you can search fields easily from the article citation to turn up similar articles. For example, suppose a particular 2005 story from the *Christian Science Monitor* suits your paper perfectly. Go to the citation and click on the subject field to find similar articles. Or, if you want to see what else the author has written, click on the author field to produce a list of articles he or she has written.

In many cases you can search the full text of articles using electronic databases and then read the entire article online. Typically, in order to use these databases you need to have a library card number or special password provided by the library. But sometimes when you use an electronic database you will find that the text of an article won't be accessible online, so you'll have to go to the library's shelves to find the magazine or newspaper in which the article originally appeared.

The *New York Times* Search by Subject Archive

Newspapers, also known as periodicals because they are issued in periodic installments (e.g., daily, weekly, or monthly), provide contemporary information. Information in periodicals—journals, magazines, and newspapers—may be useful, or even critical, when you are ready to focus in on specific aspects of your topic, or to find more up-to-date information.

There are some significant differences between newspaper articles and journal articles, and you should consider the level of scholarship that is most appropriate for your research. Popular or controversial topics may not be well covered in journals, even though coverage in newspapers and "general interest" magazines like *Newsweek* and *Science* for that same topic may be extensive.

ResearchNavigator.com gives you access to a one-year, "search by subject" archive of articles from one of the world's leading newspapers—*The New York Times*. To learn more about *The New York Times,* visit them on the Web at **http://www.nytimes.com**.

Using the search-by-subject archive is easy. Simply select a subject and type a word, or multiple words separated by commas, into the search box and click "go." The *New York Times* search by subject archive sorts article results by relevance, with the most relevant appearing first. To view the most recently published articles first, use the "Sort by" pull-down menu located just above the search results. You can further refine your search as needed. Articles can be printed or saved for later use in your research assignment. Be sure to review the citation rules for how to cite a newspaper article in endnotes or a bibliography.

"Best of the Web" Link Library

The third database included on ResearchNavigator.com, Link Library, is a collection of Web links, organized by academic subject and key terms. To use this database, simply select an academic subject from the dropdown list, and then find the key term for the topic you are searching. Click on the key term and see a list of five to seven editorially reviewed Web sites that offer educationally relevant and reliable content. For example, if your research topic is "Allergies," you may want to select the academic subject Biology and then click on "Allergies" for links to web sites that explore this topic. Simply click on the alphabet bar to view other key terms in Biology, and their corresponding links. The web links in Link Library are monitored and updated each week, reducing your incidence of finding "dead" links.

International *Financial Times* Article Archive

ResearchNavigator.com's fourth database of content is the *Financial Times* Article Archive and Company Financials Database. Through an exclusive agreement with the *Financial Times,* a leading daily newspaper covering national and international news and business, you can search this publication's one-year archive for news stories affecting countries, companies, and people throughout the world. Simply enter your keyword(s) in the text box and click the **GO** button.

Using Your Library

After you have selected your topic and gathered source material from the three databases of content on ResearchNavigator.com, you may need to complete your research by going to your school library. ResearchNavigator.com does not try to replace the library, but rather helps you understand how to use library resources effectively and efficiently.

You may put off going to the library to complete research assignments or research papers because the library can seem overwhelming. ResearchNavigator.com provides a bridge to the library by taking you through a simple step-by-step overview of how to make the most of your library time. Written by a library scientist, the *Using Your Library* tab explains:

- Major types of libraries
- What the library has to offer
- How to choose the right library tools for a project
- The research process
- How to make the most of research time in the library

In addition, when you are ready to use the library to complete a research assignment or research paper, ResearchNavigator.com includes 31 discipline-specific "library guides" for you to use as a roadmap. Each guide includes an overview of the discipline's major subject databases, online journals, and key associations and newsgroups.

For more information and detailed walk-throughs, please visit
www.researchnavigator.com/about

Start Writing

Once you've become well acquainted with the steps in the research process and gathered source materials from ResearchNavigator.com and your school library, it's time to begin writing your assignment. Content found in this tab will help you do just that, beginning with a discussion on how to draft a research paper in an academic style. Other areas addressed include:

- Blending reference material into your writing
- Writing the introduction, body, and conclusion
- Revising, proofreading, and formatting the rough draft
- Online *Grammar Guide* that spells out some of the rules and conventions of standard written English. Included are guidelines and examples for good sentence structure; tips for proper use of articles, plurals and possessives, pronouns, adjectives and adverbs; details on subject-verb agreement and verb tense consistency; and help with the various forms of punctuation.

This is also the tab where you will find sample research papers for your reference. Use them as a guide to writing your own assignment.

Endnotes & Bibliography

The final step in a research assignment is to create endnotes and a bibliography. In an era dubbed "The Information Age," knowledge and words are taking on more significance than ever. Laws requiring writers to document or give credit to the sources of information, while evolving, must be followed.

Various organizations have developed style manuals detailing how to document sources in their particular disciplines. For writing in the humanities and social sciences, the Modern Language Association (MLA) and American Psychological Association (APA) guidelines are the most commonly used, but others, such as those in *The Chicago Manual of Style* (CMS), are also required. The purpose of this Research Navigator™ tab is to help you properly cite your research sources. It contains detailed information on MLA, APA, CMS, and CBE styles. You'll also find guidance on how to cite the material you've gathered right from ResearchNavigator.com!

This Research Navigator tab also provides students with the option to use ***AutoCite.*** Students just select their documentation style (MLA or APA), and then fill in the fields with information about their source. ***AutoCite*** will do the rest! It will automatically create the entry in the proper format. Once completed, ***AutoCite*** will also generate a "Works Cited" or "References" list that students can print or save (cut and paste).

P A R T **2**

Conducting Online Research

Finding Sources: Search Engines and Subject Directories

Your professor has just given you an assignment to give a five minute speech on the topic "gun control." After a (hopefully brief) panic attack, you begin to think of what type of information you need before you can write the speech. To provide an interesting introduction, you decide to involve your class by taking a straw poll of their views for and against gun control, and to follow this up by giving some statistics on how many Americans favor (and oppose) gun control legislation and then by outlining the arguments on both sides of the issue. If you already know the correct URL for an authoritative Web site like Gallup Opinion Polls (www.gallup.com) or other sites you are in great shape! However, what do you do when you don't have a clue as to which Web site would have information on your topic? In these cases, many, many people routinely (and mistakenly) go to Yahoo! and type in a single term (e.g., guns). This approach is sure to bring first a smile to your face when the results offer you 200,874 hits on your topic, but just as quickly make you grind your teeth in frustration when you start scrolling down the hit list and find sites that range from gun dealerships, to reviews of the video "Young Guns," to aging fan sites for "Guns and Roses."

Finding information on a specific topic on the Web is a challenge. The more intricate your research need, the more difficult it is to find the one or two Web sites among the billions that feature the information you want. This section is designed to help you to avoid frustration and to focus in on the right site for your research by using search engines, subject directories, and meta-sites.

Search Engines

Search engines (sometimes called search services) are becoming more numerous on the Web. Originally, they were designed to help users search the Web by topic. More recently, search engines have added features which enhance their usefulness, such as searching a particular part of the Web (e.g., only sites of educational institutions—dot.edu), retrieving just one site which the search engine touts as most relevant (like Ask.com {www.ask.com}), or retrieving up to 10 sites which the search engine rank as most relevant (like Google {www.google.com}).

Search Engine Defined

According to Cohen (1999):

> "A search engine service provides a searchable database of Internet files collected by a computer program called a wanderer, crawler, robot, worm, or spider. Indexing is created from the collected files, and the results are presented in a schematic order. There are no selection criteria for the collection of files.
>
> A search service therefore consists of three components: (1) a spider, a program that traverses the Web from link to link, identifying and reading pages; (2) an index, a database containing a copy of each Web page gathered by the spider; and (3) a search engine mechanism, software that enables users to query the index and then returns results in a schematic order (p. 31)."

One problem students often have in their use of search engines is that they are deceptively easy to use. Like our example "guns," no matter what is typed into the handy box at the top, links to numerous Web sites appear instantaneously, lulling students into a false sense of security. Since so much was retrieved, surely SOME of it must be useful. WRONG! Many Web sites retrieved will be very light on substantive content, which is not what you need for most academic endeavors. Finding just the right Web site has been likened to finding diamonds in the desert.

As you can see by the definition above, one reason for this is that most search engines use indexes developed by machines. Therefore they are indexing terms not concepts. The search engine cannot tell the difference between the keyword "crack" to mean a split in the sidewalk and "crack" referring to crack cocaine. To use search engines properly takes some skill, and this chapter will provide tips to help you use search engines more effectively. First, however, let's look at the different types of search engines with examples:

TYPES OF SEARCH ENGINES

TYPE	DESCRIPTION	EXAMPLES
1st Generation	• Non-evaluative, do not evaluate results in terms of content or authority. • Return results ranked by relevancy alone (number of times the term(s) entered appear, usually on the first paragraph or page of the site)	AltaVista (www.altavista.com) Excite (www.excite.com) HotBot (www.HotBot.com) Ixquick Metasearch (ixquick.com) Lycos (www.lycos.com)
2nd Generation	• More creative in displaying results. • Results are ordered by characteristics such as: concept, document type, Web site, popularity, etc. rather than relevancy.	Ask (www.ask.com) Direct Hit (www.directhit.com) Google! (www.google.com) HotLinks (www.hotlinks.com) Simplifind (www.simpli.com) SurfWax (www.surfwax.com) Also see Meta-Search engines below. EVALUATIVE SEARCH ENGINES About.Com (www.about.com) WebCrawler (www.webcrawler.com)
Commercial Portals	• Provide additional features such as: customized news, stock quotations, weather reports, shopping, etc. • They want to be used as a "one stop" Web guide. • They profit from prominent advertisements and fees charged to featured sites.	GONetwork (www.go.com) Google Web Directory (directory.google.com) LookSmart (www.looksmart.com) My Starting Point (www.stpt.com) Open Directory Project (dmoz.org) NetNow (www.inetnow.com) Yahoo! (www.yahoo.com)
Meta-Search Engines	Run searches on multiple search engines.	There are different types of meta-search engines. See the next 2 boxes.

(continued)

TYPES OF SEARCH ENGINES, *continued*

TYPE	DESCRIPTION	EXAMPLES
Meta-Search Engines *Integrated Result*	• Display results for search engines in one list. • Duplicates are removed. • Only portions of results from each engine are returned.	Beaucoup.com (www.beaucoup.com) Highway 61 (www.highway61.com) Cyber411 (www.cyber411. com) Mamma (www.mamma.com) MetaCrawler (www. metacrawler.com) Visisimo (www.vivisimo.com) Northern Light (www.nlsearch.com) SurfWax (www.surfwax.com)
Meta-Search Engines *Non-Integrated Results*	• Comprehensive search. • Displays results from each search engine in separate results sets. • Duplicates remain. • You must sift through all the sites.	Dogpile (www.dogpile.com) GoHip (www.gohip.com) Searchalot (www.searchalot.com) ProFusion (www. profusion.com)

QUICK TIPS FOR MORE EFFECTIVE USE OF SEARCH ENGINES

1. Use a search engine:
   - When you have a narrow idea to search.
   - When you want to search the full text of countless Web pages
   - When you want to retrieve a large number of sites
   - When the features of the search engine (like searching particular parts of the Web) help with your search

2. Always use Boolean Operators to combine terms. Searching on a single term is a sure way to retrieve a very large number of Web pages, few, if any, of which are on target.
   - Always check search engine's HELP feature to see what symbols are used for the operators as these vary (e.g., some engines use the & or + symbol for AND).
   - Boolean Operators include:
     AND to narrow search and to make sure that **both** terms are included
       e.g., children AND violence
     OR to broaden search and to make sure that **either** term is included
       e.g., child OR children OR juveniles
     NOT to **exclude** one term
       e.g., eclipse NOT lunar

3. Use appropriate symbols to indicate important terms and to indicate phrases (Best Bet for Constructing a Search According to Cohen (1999): Use a plus sign (+) in front of terms you want to retrieve: +solar +eclipse. Place a phrase in double quotation marks: "solar eclipse" Put together: "+solar eclipse" "+South America").

4. Use word stemming (a.k.a. truncation) to find all variations of a word (check search engine HELP for symbols).
   • If you want to retrieve child, child's, or children use child* (some engines use other symbols such as !, #, or $)
   • Some engines automatically search singular and plural terms, check HELP to see if yours does.

5. Since search engines only search a portion of the Web, use several search engines or a meta-search engine to extend your reach.

6. Remember search engines are generally mindless drones that do not evaluate. Do not rely on them to find the best Web sites on your topic, use *subject directories* or meta-sites to enhance value (see below).

Finding Those Diamonds in the Desert: Using Subject Directories and Meta-sites

Although some search engines, like WebCrawler (www.webcrawler.com) do evaluate the Web sites they index, most search engines do not make any judgment on the worth of the content. They just return a long—sometimes very long—list of sites that contained your keyword. However, *subject directories* exist that are developed by human indexers, usually librarians or subject experts, and are defined by Cohen (1999) as follows:

> "A subject directory is a service that offers a collection of links to Internet resources submitted by site creators or evaluators and organized into subject categories. Directory services use selection criteria for choosing links to include, though the selectivity varies among services (p. 27)."

World Wide Web Subject directories are useful when you want to see sites on your topic that have been reviewed, evaluated, and selected for their authority, accuracy, and value. They can be real time savers for students, since subject directories weed out the commercial, lightweight, or biased Web sites.

Metasites are similar to subject directories, but are more specific in nature, usually dealing with one scholarly field or discipline. Some examples of subject directories and meta-sites are found in the table on the next page.

SMART SEARCHING—SUBJECT DIRECTORIES AND META-SITES

TYPES—SUBJECT DIRECTORIES	EXAMPLES
General, covers many topics	Access to Internet and Subject Resources (www2.lib.udel.edu/subj/)
	Best Information on the Net (BIOTN) (http://library.sau.edu/bestinfo/)
	INFOMINE: Scholarly Internet Resource Collections (http://infomine.ucr.edu/)
	Librarian's Index to the Internet (www.lii.org/)
	Martindale's "The Reference Desk" (www.martindalecenter.com)
	PINAKES: A Subject Launchpad (www.hw.ac.uk/libWWW/irn/pinakes/pinakes.html)
	Refdesk.com (www.refdesk.com)
	Search Engines and Subject Directories (College of New Jersey) (www.tcnj.edu/~library/research/internet_search.html)
	Scout Report Archives (www.scout.cs.wisc.edu/archives)
	WWW Virtual Library (http://vlib.org)
Subject Oriented	
• Communication Studies	The Media and Communication Studies Site (www.aber.ac.uk/media)
	University of Iowa Department of Communication Studies (www.uiowa.edu/~commstud/resources)
• Cultural Studies	Sara Zupko's Cultural Studies Center (www.popcultures.com)
• Education	Educational Virtual Library (www.csu.edu.au/education/library.html)
	ERIC [Education ResourcesInformation Center] (www.eduref.org)
	Kathy Schrock's Guide for Educators (http://kathyschrock.net/abceval/index.htm)
• Journalism	Journalism Resources (https://bailiwick.lib.uiowa.edu/journalism/)
	Journalism and Media Criticism page (www.chss.montclair.edu/english/furr/media.html)
• Literature	Norton Web Source to American Literature (www.wwnorton.com/naal)
	Project Gutenberg [Over 3,000 full text titles] (www.gutenberg.org)

SMART SEARCHING, *continued*

TYPES—SUBJECT DIRECTORIES	EXAMPLES
• Medicine & Health	PubMed [National Library of Medicine's index to Medical journals, 1966 to present] (www.ncbi.nlm.nih.gov/PubMed/) RxList: The Internet Drug Index (http://rxlist.com) Go Ask Alice (www.goaskalice.columbia.edu) [Health and sexuality]
• Technology	CNET.com (www.cnet.com)

Choose subject directories to ensure that you are searching the highest quality Web pages. As an added bonus, subject directories periodically check Web links to make sure that there are fewer dead ends and out-dated links.

Another closely related group of sites are the *Virtual Library sites,* also referred to as Digital Library sites (see the table below). Hopefully, your campus library has an outstanding Web site for both on-campus and off-campus access to resources. If not, there are

VIRTUAL LIBRARY SITES

PUBLIC LIBRARIES

• Internet Public Library	www.ipl.org
• Library of Congress	http://lcweb.loc.gov/homepage/lchp.html
• New York Public Library	www.nypl.org

University/College Libraries	
• Case Western	www.cwru.edu/uclibraries.html
• Dartmouth	www.dartmouth.edu/~library
• Duke	www.lib.duke.edu/
• Franklin & Marshall	www.library.fandm.edu
• Harvard	www.harvard.edu/museums/
• Penn State	www.libraries.psu.edu
• Stanford	www.slac.stanford.edu/FIND/spires.html
• ULCA	www.library.ucla.edu

Other	
• Perseus Project [subject specific—classics, supported by grants from corporations and educational institutions]	www.perseus.tufts.edu

several virtual library sites that you can use, although you should realize that some of the resources would be subscription based, and not accessible unless you are a student of that particular university or college. These are useful because, like the subject directories and meta-sites, experts have organized Web sites by topic and selected only those of highest quality.

You now know how to search for information and use search engines more effectively. In the next section, you will learn more tips for evaluating the information that you found.

BIBLIOGRAPHY FOR FURTHER READING

Books

Basch, Reva. (1996). *Secrets of the Super Net Searchers.*

Berkman, Robert I. (2000). *Find It Fast: How to Uncover Expert Information on Any Subject Online or in Print.* NY: HarperResource.

Glossbrenner, Alfred & Glossbrenner, Emily. (1999). *Search Engines for the World Wide Web,* 2nd Ed. Berkeley, CA: Peachpit Press.

Hock, Randolph, & Berinstein, Paula. (1999). *The Extreme Searcher's Guide to Web Search Engines: A Handbook for the Serious Searcher.* Information Today, Inc.

Miller, Michael. (2000). *Complete Idiot's Guide to Yahoo!* Indianapolis, IN: Que.

Miller, Michael. (2000). *Complete Idiot's Guide to Online Search Secrets.* Indianapolis, IN: Que.

Paul, Nora, Williams, Margot, & Hane, Paula. (1999). *Great Scouts!: Cyber-Guides for Subject Searching on the Web.* Information Today, Inc.

Radford, Marie, Barnes, Susan, & Barr, Linda. (2001). *Web Research: Selecting, Evaluating, and Citing* Boston. Allyn and Bacon.

Journal Articles

Cohen, Laura B. (1999, August). The Web as a research tool: Teaching strategies for instructors. *CHOICE Supplement* 3, 20–44.

Cohen, Laura B. (August 2000). Searching the Web: The Human Element Emerges. *CHOICE Supplement 37,* 17–31.

Introna, Lucas D., & Nissenbaum, Helen. (2000). Shaping the web: Why the politics of search engines matters. The Information Society, Vol. 16, No. 3, pp. 169–185.

Evaluating Sources on the Web

Congratulations! You've found a great Web site. Now what? The Web site you found seems like the perfect Web site for your research.

But, are you sure? Why is it perfect? What criteria are you using to determine whether this Web site suits your purpose?

Think about it. Where else on earth can anyone "publish" information regardless of the *accuracy, currency,* or *reliability* of the information? The Internet has opened up a world of opportunity for posting and distributing information and ideas to virtually everyone, even those who might post misinformation for fun, or those with ulterior motives for promoting their point of view. Armed with the information provided in this guide, you can dig through the vast amount of useless information and misinformation on the World Wide Web to uncover the valuable information. Because practically anyone can post and distribute their ideas on the Web, you need to develop a new set of *critical thinking skills* that focus on the evaluation of the quality of information, rather than be influenced and manipulated by slick graphics and flashy moving java script.

Before the existence of online sources, the validity and accuracy of a source was more easily determined. For example, in order for a book to get to the publishing stage, it must go through many critiques, validation of facts, reviews, editorial changes and the like. Ownership of the information in the book is clear because the author's name is attached to it. The publisher's reputation is on the line too. If the book turns out to have incorrect information, reputations and money can be lost. In addition, books available in a university library are further reviewed by professional librarians and selected for library purchase because of their accuracy and value to students. Journal articles downloaded or printed from online subscription services, such as Infotrac, ProQuest, EbscoHost, or other fulltext databases, are put through the same scrutiny as the paper versions of the journals.

On the World Wide Web, however, Internet service providers (ISPs) simply give Web site authors a place to store information. The Web site author can post information that may not be validated or tested for accuracy. One mistake students typically make is to assume that all information on the Web is of equal value. Also, in the rush to get assignments in on time, students may not take the extra time to make sure that the information they are citing is accurate. It is easy just to cut and paste without really thinking about the content in a critical way. However, to make sure you are gathering accurate information and to get the best grade on your assignments, it is vital that you develop your critical ability to sift through the dirt to find the diamonds.

Web Evaluation Criteria

So, here you are, at this potentially great site. Let's go though some ways you can determine if this site is one you can cite with confidence in your research. Keep in mind, ease of use of a Web site is an

Evaluating Web Sites Using
Five Criteria to Judge Web Site Content

Accuracy—How reliable is the information?

Authority—Who is the author and what are his or her credentials?

Objectivity—Does the Web site present a balanced or biased point of view?

Coverage—Is the information comprehensive enough for your needs?

Currency—Is the Web site up to date?

Use additional criteria to judge Web site content, including

- **Publisher, documentation, relevance, scope, audience, appropriateness of format,** and **navigation**
- Judging whether the site is made up of **primary (original) or secondary (interpretive) sources**
- Determining whether the information is **relevant** to your research

issue, but more important is learning how to determine the validity of data, facts, and statements for your use. The five traditional ways to verify a paper source can also be applied to your Web source: *accuracy, authority, objectivity, coverage,* and *currency.*

Content Evaluation

Accuracy.   Internet searches are not the same as searches of library databases because much of the information on the Web has not been edited, whereas information in databases has. It is your responsibility to make sure that the information you use in a school project is accurate. When you examine the content on a Web site or Web page, you can ask yourself a number of questions to determine whether the information is accurate.

1. Is the information reliable?
2. Do the facts from your other research contradict the facts you find on this Web page?
3. Do any misspellings and/or grammar mistakes indicate a hastily put together Web site that has not been checked for accuracy?
4. Is the content on the page verifiable through some other source? Can you find similar facts elsewhere (journals, books, or other online sources) to support the facts you see on this Web page?
5. Do you find links to other Web sites on a similar topic? If so, check those links to ascertain whether they back up the information you see on the Web page you are interested in using.
6. Is a bibliography of additional sources for research provided? Lack of a bibliography doesn't mean the page isn't accurate, but

having one allows you further investigation points to check the information.

7. Does the site of a research document or study explain how the data was collected and the type of research method used to interpret the data?

If you've found a site with information that seems too good to be true, it may be. You need to verify information that you read on the Web by crosschecking against other sources.

Authority.   An important question to ask when you are evaluating a Web site is, "Who is the author of the information?" Do you know whether the author is a recognized authority in his or her field? Biographical information, references to publications, degrees, qualifications, and organizational affiliations can help to indicate an author's authority. For example, if you are researching the topic of laser surgery citing a medical doctor would be better than citing a college student who has had laser surgery.

The organization sponsoring the site can also provide clues about whether the information is fact or opinion. Examine how the information was gathered and the research method used to prepare the study or report. Other questions to ask include:

1. Who is responsible for the content of the page? Although a webmaster's name is often listed, this person is not necessarily responsible for the content.
2. Is the author recognized in the subject area? Does this person cite any other publications he or she has authored?
3. Does the author list his or her background or credentials (e.g., Ph.D. degree, title such as professor, or other honorary or social distinction)?
4. Is there a way to contact the author? Does the author provide a phone number or email address?
5. If the page is mounted by an organization, is it a known, reputable one?
6. How long has the organization been in existence?
7. Does the URL for the Web page end in the extension .edu or .org? Such extensions indicate authority compared to dotcoms (.com), which are commercial enterprises. (For example, www.cancer.com takes you to an online drugstore that has a cancer information page; www.cancer.org is the American Cancer Society Web site.)

A good idea is to ask yourself whether the author or organization presenting the information on the Web is an authority on the subject. If the answer is no, this may not be a good source of information.

Objectivity.   Every author has a point of view, and some views are more controversial than others. Journalists try to be objective by providing both sides of a story. Academics attempt to persuade readers by presenting a logical argument, which cites other scholars' work. You need to look for two sided arguments in news and information sites. For academic papers, you need to determine how the paper fits within its discipline and whether the author is using controversial methods for reporting a conclusion.

Authoritative authors situate their work within a larger discipline. This background helps readers evaluate the author's knowledge on a particular subject. You should ascertain whether the author's approach is controversial and whether he or she acknowledges this. More important, is the information being presented as fact or opinion? Authors who argue for their position provide readers with other sources that support their arguments. If no sources are cited, the material may be an opinion piece rather than an objective presentation of information. The following questions can help you determine objectivity:

1. Is the purpose of the site clearly stated, either by the author or the organization authoring the site?
2. Does the site give a balanced viewpoint or present only one side?
3. Is the information directed toward a specific group of viewers?
4. Does the site contain advertising?
5. Does the copyright belong to a person or an organization?
6. Do you see anything to indicate who is funding the site?

Everyone has a point of view. This is important to remember when you are using Web resources. A question to keep asking yourself is, What is the bias or point of *view* being expressed here?

Coverage.   Coverage deals with the breadth and depth of information presented on a Web site. Stated another way, it is about how much information is presented and how detailed the information is. Looking at the site map or index can give you an idea about how much information is contained on a site. This isn't necessarily bad. Coverage is a criteria that is tied closely to *your* research requirement. For one assignment, a given Web site may be too general for your needs. For another assignment, that same site might be perfect. Some sites contain very little actual information because pages are filled with links to other sites. Coverage also relates to objectivity. You should ask the following questions about coverage:

1. Does the author present both sides of the story or is a piece of the story missing?

2. Is the information comprehensive enough for your needs?
3. Does the site cover too much, too generally?
4. Do you need more specific information than the site can provide?
5. Does the site have an objective approach?

In addition to examining what is covered on a Web site, equally revealing is what is not covered. Missing information can reveal a bias in the material. Keep in mind that you are evaluating the information on a Web site for your research requirements.

Currency.   Currency questions deal with the timeliness of information. However, currency is more important for some topics than for others. For example, currency is essential when you are looking for technology related topics and current events. In contrast, currency may not be relevant when you are doing research on Plato or Ancient Greece. In terms of Web sites, currency also pertains to whether the site is being kept up to date and links are being maintained. Sites on the Web are sometimes abandoned by their owners. When people move or change jobs, they may neglect to remove theft site from the company or university server. To test currency ask the following questions:

1. Does the site indicate when the content was created?
2. Does the site contain a last revised date? How old is the date? (In the early part of 2001, a university updated their Web site with a "last updated" date of 1901! This obviously was a Y2K problem, but it does point out the need to be observant of such things!)
3. Does the author state how often he or she revises the information? Some sites are on a monthly update cycle (e.g., a government statistics page).
4. Can you tell specifically what content was revised?
5. Is the information still useful for your topic? Even if the last update is old, the site might still be worthy of use *if* the content is still valid for your research.

Relevancy to Your Research: Primary versus Secondary Sources

Some research assignments require the use of primary (original) sources. Materials such as raw data, diaries, letters, manuscripts, and original accounts of events can be considered primary material. In most cases, these historical documents are no longer copyrighted. The Web is a great source for this type of resource.

Information that has been analyzed and previously interpreted is considered a secondary source. Sometimes secondary sources are more appropriate than primary sources. If, for example, you are asked to analyze a topic or to find an analysis of a topic, a secondary source of an analysis would be most appropriate. Ask yourself the following questions to determine whether the Web site is relevant to your research:

1. Is it a primary or secondary source?
2. Do you need a primary source?
3. Does the assignment require you to cite different types of sources? For example, are you supposed to use at least one book, one journal article, and one Web page?

You need to think critically, both visually and verbally, when evaluating Web sites. Because Web sites are designed as multimedia hypertexts, nonlinear texts, visual elements, and navigational tools are added to the evaluation process.

Help in Evaluating Web Sites.   One shortcut to finding high-quality Web sites is using subject directories and meta-sites, which select the Web sites they index by similar evaluation criteria to those just described. If you want to learn more about evaluating Web sites, many colleges and universities provide sites that help you evaluate Web resources. The following list contains some excellent examples of these evaluation sites:

- Evaluating Quality on the Net—Hope Tillman, Babson College
  www.hopetillman.com/findqual.html
- Critical Web Evaluation—Kurt W. Wagner, William Paterson University of New Jersey
  http://euphrates.wpunj.edu/faculty/wagnerk/
- Evalation Criteria—Susan Beck, New Mexico State University
  http://lib.nmsu.edu/instruction/evalcrit.html
- A Student's Guide to Research with the WWW
  www.slu.edu/departments/english/research/

Critical Evaluation Web Sites

WEB SITE AND URL	SOURCE
Critical Thinking in an Online World **www.library.ucsb.edu/untangle/** **jones.html**	*Paper from "Untangling the Web" 1996*
Educom Review: Information **www.educause.edu/pub/er/review/** **reviewArticles/31231.html**	*EDUCAUSE Literacy as a Liberal Art (1996 article)*

WEB SITE AND URL	SOURCE
Evaluating Web Sites www.lib.purdue.edu/InternetEval	*Purdue University Library*
Searching the Web www.lehigh.edu/helpdesk/ useweb.html	*Lehigh University*
Kathy Schrock's ABC's of Web Site Evaluation www.kathyschrock.net/abceval/	*Author's Web site*
Testing the Surf: Criteria for Evaluating Internet Information Sources http://info.lib.uh.edu/pr/v8/n3/ smit8n3.html	*University of Houston Libraries*
UCLA College Library Instruction: Thinking Critically about World Wide Web Resources www.library.ucla.edu/libraries/ college/help/critical/	*UCLA Library*
UG OOL: Judging Quality on the Internet www.open.uoguelph.ca/resources/ skills/judging.html	*University of Guelph*
Web Evaluation Criteria http://lib.nmsu.edu/instruction/ evalcrit.html	*New Mexico State University Library*
Web Page Credibility Checklist www.park.pvt.k12.md.us/academics/ research/credcheck.htm	*Park School of Baltimore*
Evaluating Web Sites for Educational Uses: Bibliography and Checklist www.unc.edu/cit/guides/irg-49.html	*University of North Carolina*
Evaluating Web Sites www.lesley.edu/library/guides/ research/evaluating_web.html	*Lesley University*

Tip: Can't seem to get a URL to work? If the URL doesn't begin with www, you may need to put the http:// in front of the URL. Usually, browsers can handle URLs that begin with www without the need to type in the "http://" but if you find you're having trouble, add the http://.

Documentation Guidelines for Online Sources

Your Citation for Exemplary Research

There's another detail left for us to handle—the formal citing of electronic sources in academic papers. The very factor that makes research on the Internet exciting is the same factor that makes referencing these sources challenging: their dynamic nature. A journal article exists, either in print or on microfilm, virtually forever. A document on the Internet can come, go, and change without warning. Because the purpose of citing sources is to allow another scholar to retrace your argument, a good citation allows a reader to obtain information from your primary sources, to the extent possible. This means you need to include not only information on when a source was posted on the Internet (if available) but also when you obtained the information.

The two arbiters of form for academic and scholarly writing are the Modern Language Association (MLA) and the American Psychological Association (APA); both organizations have established styles for citing electronic publications.

MLA Style

In the fifth edition of the *MLA Handbook for Writers of Research Papers,* the MLA recommends the following formats:

- **URLs:** URLs are enclosed in angle brackets (<>) and contain the access mode identifier, the formal name for such indicators as "http" or "ftp." If a URL must be split across two lines, break it only after a slash (/). Never introduce a hyphen at the end of the first line. The URL should include all the parts necessary to identify uniquely the file/document being cited.

  `<http://www.csun.edu/~rtvfdept/home/index.html>`

- **An online scholarly project or reference database:** A complete "online reference contains the title of the project or database (underlined); the name of the editor of the project or database (if given); electronic publication information, including version number (if relevant and if not part of the title), date of electronic publication or latest update, and name of any sponsoring institution or organization; date of access; and electronic address.

  <u>The Perseus Project</u>. Ed. Gregory R. Crane.
  Mar. 1997. Department of Classics,
  Tufts University. 15 June 1998 <http://
  www.perseus.tufts.edu/>.

If you cannot find some of the information, then include the information that is available. The MLA also recommends that you print or download electronic documents, freezing them in time for future reference.

- **A document within a scholarly project or reference database:** It is much more common to use only a portion of a scholarly project or database. To cite an essay, poem, or other short work, begin this citation with the name of the author and the title of the work (in quotation marks). Then, include all the information used when citing a complete online scholarly project or reference database, however, make sure you use the URL of the specific work and not the address of the general site.

Cuthberg, Lori. "Moonwalk: Earthlings' Finest
   Hour." <u>Discovery Channel Online</u>. 1999.
   Discovery Channel. 25 Nov. 1999 <http://
   www.discovery.com/indep/newsfeatures/
   moonwalk/challenge.html>.

- **A professional or personal site:** Include the name of the person creating the site (reversed), followed by a period, the title of the site (underlined), or, if there is no title, a description such as Home page (such a description is neither placed in quotes nor underlined). Then, specify the name of any school, organization, or other institution affiliated with the site and follow it with your date of access and the URL of the page.

Packer, Andy. Home page. 1Apr. 1998 <http://
   www.suu.edu/~students/Packer.htm>.

Some electronic references are truly unique to the online domain. These include email, newsgroup postings, MUDs (multiuser domains) or MOOs (multiuser domains, object-oriented), and IRCs (Internet Relay Chats).

   Email. In citing email messages, begin with the writer's name (reversed) followed by a period, then the title of the message (if any) in quotations as it appears in the subject line. Next comes a description of the message, typically "Email to," and the recipient (e.g., "the author"), and finally the date of the message.

Davis, Jeffrey. "Web Writing Resources." Email
   to Nora Davis. 3 Jan. 2000.

Sommers, Laurice. "Re: College Admissions Prac-
   tices." Email to the author. 12 Aug. 1998.

List Servers and Newsgroups. In citing these references, begin with the author's name (reversed) followed by a period. Next include the title of the document (in quotes) from the subject line, followed by the words "Online posting" (not in quotes). Follow this with the date of posting. For list servers, include the date of access, the name of the list (if known), and the online address of the list's moderator or administrator. For newsgroups, follow "Online posting" with the date of posting, the date of access, and the name of the newsgroup, prefixed with "news:" and enclosed in angle brackets.

Applebaum, Dale. "Educational Variables." Online
    posting. 29 Jan. 1998. Higher Education Dis-
    cussion Group. 30 Jan. 1993 <jlucidoj@unc.edu>.

Gostl, Jack. "Re: Mr. Levitan." Online posting.
    13 June 1997. 20 June 1997 <news:alt.edu.
    bronxscience>.

MUDs, MOOs, and IRCs. Begin with the name of the speaker(s) followed by a period. Follow with the description and date of the event, the forum in which the communication took place, the date of access, and the online address. If you accessed the MOO or MUD through telnet, your citation might appear as follows:

Guest. Personal interview. 13 Aug. 1998.
    <telnet://du.edu:8888>.

For more information on MLA documentation style for online sources, check out their Web site at http://www.mla.org/style/sources.htm.

APA Style

The newly revised *Publication Manual of the American Psychological Association* (5th ed.) now includes guidelines for Internet resources. The manual recommends that, at a minimum, a reference of an Internet source should provide a document title or description, a date (either the date of publication or update or the date of retrieval), and an address (in Internet terms, a uniform resource locator, or URL). Whenever possible, identify the authors of a document as well. It's important to remember that, unlike the MLA, the APA does not include temporary or transient sources (e.g., letters, phone calls, etc.) in its "References" page, preferring to handle them in the text. The general suggested format is as follows:

Online periodical:

Author, A. A., Author, B. B., & Author,
C. C. (2000). Title of article. *Title of
Periodical, xx*, xxxxx. Retrieved month, day,
year, from source.

Online document:

Author, A. A. (2000). *Title of work*. Retrieved
month, day, year, from source.

Some more specific examples are as follows:

FTP (File Transfer Protocol) Sites. To cite files available for downloading via FTP, give the author's name (if known), the publication date (if available and if different from the date accessed), the full title of the paper (capitalizing only the first word and proper nouns), the date of access, and the address of the FTP site along with the full path necessary to access the file.

Deutsch, P. (1991) Archie: An electronic
directory service for the Internet. Retrieved
January 25, 2000 from File Transfer Protocol:
ftp://ftp.sura.net/pub/archie/docs/
whatis.archie

WWW Sites (World Wide Web). To cite files available for viewing or downloading via the World Wide Web, give the author's name (if known), the year of publication (if known and if different from the date accessed), the full title of the article, and the title of the complete work (if applicable) in italics. Include any additional information (such as versions, editions, or revisions) in parentheses immediately following the title. Include the date of retrieval and full URL (the http address).

Burka, L. P. (1993). A hypertext history of
multi-user dungeons. *MUDdex*. Retrieved
January 13, 1997 from the World Wide Web:
http://www.utopia.com/talent/lpb/muddex/essay/

Tilton, J. (1995). Composing good HTML (Vers.
2.0.6). Retrieved December 1, 1996 from the
World Wide Web: http://www.cs.cmu.edu/
~tilt/cgh/

Synchronous Communications (MOOs, MUDs, IRC, etc.). Give the name of the speaker(s), the complete date of the conversation being referenced in parentheses, and the title of the session (if applicable). Next, list the title of the site in italics, the protocol and address (if applicable), and any directions necessary to access the work. Last, list the date of access, followed by the retrieval information. Personal interviews do not need to be listed in the References, but do need to be included in parenthetic references in the text (see the APA *Publication Manual*).

Cross, J. (1996, February 27). Netoric's Tuesday "cafe: Why use MUDs in the writing classroom? *MediaMoo*. Retrieved March 1, 1996 from File Transfer Protocol: ftp://daedalus.com/pub/ ACW/NETORIC/catalog

Gopher Sites. List the author's name (if applicable), the year of publication, the title of the file or paper, and the title of the complete work (if applicable). Include any print publication information (if available) followed by the protocol (i.e., gopher://). List the date that the file was accessed and the path necessary to access the file.

Massachusetts Higher Education Coordinating Council. (1994). Using coordination and collaboration to address change. Retrieved July 16, 1999 from the World Wide Web: gopher://gopher.mass.edu:170/ 00gopher_root%3A%5B_hecc%5D_plan

Email, Listservs, and Newsgroups. Do not include personal email in the list of References. Although unretrievable communication such as email is not included in APA References, somewhat more public or accessible Internet postings from newsgroups or listservs may be included. See the APA *Publication Manual* for information on in-text citations.

Heilke, J. (1996, May 3). Webfolios. Alliance for Computers and Writing Discussion List. Retrieved December 31, 1996 from the World Wide Web: http://www.ttu.edu/lists/acw-l/ 9605/0040.html

Other authors and educators have proposed similar extensions to the APA style. You can find links to these pages at:

www.psychwww.com/resource/apacrib.htm

Remember, "frequently-referenced" does not equate to "correct" "or even "desirable." Check with your professor to see if your course or school has a preference for an extended APA style.

PART 3

Research Tips for Sociology

The field of sociology is very broad, extending over a wide range of human behavior and concerns. The research literature in sociology is therefore very extensive, with dozens of general and specialized, scholarly periodicals. To use the Research Navigator productively, you must first define the research topic or question precisely. If your initial search produces hundreds of citations, either the topic you chose is too broad, or the search terms you selected are too general. If your initial search produces no, or too few, citations, you need to expand your topic or your search terms.

Sample Searches

Two examples of searches are presented here to demonstrate the process of refining the choice of search terms and identifying additional resources as the results of the search unfold.

Example #1: The first example is a search on the topic "problems encountered by people growing old in America." The first step is to select search terms that are likely to produce "hits" in the online databases that are focused on the topic of interest. A vast array of materials unrelated to the topic of interest would be called up by searching on a term that is too general, like "age." For example, searching the *New York Times* Subject Archive with the term "age" produces a list of 246 articles, most of which are unrelated to our topic.

Choosing search terms that are general enough to cover the topic but specific enough to exclude unrelated material is an important component of every successful search strategy. "Aging" (i.e., the process of growing older) and "ageism" (i.e., prejudice and discrimination on the basis of age) are likely search terms. Here are the results of searches, using those terms, in three online databases accessible from Research Navigator.com.

ContentSelect Academic Journals

Searching with the term "aging" produced too many (i.e., 436) sources, most of which were not useful. Searching with "problems of aging," on the other hand, produced just one source. Combining "problems" with "aging" (i.e., searching on the phrase, "problems and aging" seemed to work best, producing 24 articles, nearly all of which covered issues related to our topic. The article titles and sources are listed below. Clicking on each title on your screen will lead to the full text and citation of each article:

• An Anti-Alzheimer's Workout. *U.S. News & World Report.*
• The Value of Telephone Support Groups Among Ethnically Diverse Caregiver's of Persons With Dementia. *Gerontologist.*
• BOOKS RECEIVED. *Gerontologist.*
• The Self and Mental Health: Self-Salience and the Emergence of Internalizing and Externalizing Problems. *Journal of Health & Social Behavior.*
• Determinants of Mortality at Older Ages: The Role of Biological Markers of Chronic Disease. *Population & Development Review.*
• D. V. Glass on the Problems of a Declining Population. *Population & Development Review.*
• Using Remote Assessment to Provide Home Modification Services to Underserved Elders. *Gerontologist.*
• INSIGHTS FROM A CANADIAN SEXUALITY CONFERENCE: REFLECTIONS OF A MIDWIFE FROM IRAN. *Canadian Journal of Human Sexuality.*
• Katherine Kendall: A Social Work Institution. *Journal of Women & Social Work.*
• Acceptability of less than perfect health states. *Social Science & Medicine.*

- A nation's wake-up call. *U.S. News & World Report.*
- Reasons Given by Older People for Limitation or Avoidance of Driving. *Gerontologist.*
- The good, the bad, and the unresolved death in Kaliai. *Social Science & Medicine.*
- A story of maladies, misconceptions and mishaps: effective management of heart failure. *Social Science & Medicine.*
- Sentence Completion to Assess Children's Views About Aging. *Gerontologist.*
- The process of mediated aging-in-place: a theoretically and empirically based model. *Social Science & Medicine.*
- GRID LOCK. *U.S. News & World Report.*
- From home to hospital and back again: economic restructuring, end of life, and the gendered problems of place-switching health services. *Social Science & Medicine.*
- Finding the Best Ways to Help: Opportunities and Challenges of Intervention Research on Aging. *Gerontologist.*
- The effect of social relations with children on the education–health link in men and women aged 40 and over. *Social Science & Medicine.*
- Automated telephone answering systems and aging. *Behaviour & Information Technology.*
- New Book Explores Problems of Health Coverage and Income Security of Aging Workforce. *Human Ecology.*
- The End of the Demographic Transition: Relief or Concern? *Population & Development Review.*
- Learning to Be More Hopeful and Resilient. *Newsweek.*

Examining the sources of articles produced by this search offers hints at other potentially productive search strategies, in addition to online databases. Note that the search in the ContentSelect Academic Journals database produced several articles from three specific academic journals (i.e., *Social Science and Medicine, Population & Development Review,* and *The Gerontologist*). Other issues of these three journals are likely to contain more articles relevant to the topic under investigation. Abstracts and full-text versions of many academic journals are available online, typically through academic library subscriptions. The student may therefore wish to search these journals, either online, if they are accessible through the student's college or university library, or in printed form in the library.

New York Times Archive

Selecting "Sociology" from the *New York Times* Archive Search Menu, and searching on the term "aging" produced the eleven articles whose headlines are reproduced below. Clicking on a headline reveals the full text of the article:

- Aging at Home: For a Lucky Few, a Wish Come True
- Aging in City Easily Beats Other Options
- Need Turns Aging Strangers Into Roommates
- Aging: Benefits Abound for Heart Surgery After 80
- Aging and Infirmity Are Twinned No Longer
- Aging, Frail, and Now Refugees From a Devastating Hurricane
- Aging: Dementia Is Linked to Blood Flow to the Brain
- Aging: Clues for the 'Stay Sharp' Diet
- Sharing and Apart, as a Life Ebbs (5 Letters)
- Older, but Not Isolated
- It Can Be Done: Scientists Teach Old Dogs New Tricks

"Best of the Web" Link Library

This database of useful Web links can be searched using the same or similar search terms as with the other databases. Instead of listing published articles, however, the "Best of the Web" resource offers links to organizations and other information sources on the Web.

After selecting the subject "sociology" in the Link Library search window, clicking on the topic "Aging/Ageism" reveals the a list of public Web sites, listed here along with brief descriptions. Clicking on the name of a Web site will take your browser to that Web site:

Social Gerontology and the Aging Revolution—An extensive exploration of sociological aspects of aging, with access to related sites available for viewing.

National Institute on Aging—The National Institute on Aging's home page, providing access to current information and research on health and aging.

American Association of Retired People (AARP)—Homepage for the national organization for people age 50 and older.

ADEA—Full text of the 1967 Age Discrimination in Employment Act; site maintained by the Equal Employment Opportunity Commission (EEOC).

Administration on Aging—The Administration on Aging's home page, offering education resources, including statistical information.

GeroWeb—Wayne State University provides this online resource for those interested in the topic of aging.

Ageism in the Preclinical Years—Sponsored by the Journal of the American Medical Association, this article, written by a medical school student, discusses ageism in medical students.

Many Web links may be followed to reveal other, more detailed information, including authoritative, current information on a topic. For example, clicking on the **National Institute on Aging** Web link, leads your browser to a page that offers, among the links under "Health Information," a "Publications" link. Following that link leads to a page that lists "Healthy Aging." In turn, that page lists both links to full-text articles and other materials that can be ordered from the NIA. Similarly, the **Administration on Aging** Web link leads to a rich source of news items on current government policies that impact the lives of older people.

Example #2—The second example of a Research Navigator Web search is on the topic, "What is the relationship between recreational drug use and other types of crimes?" Developing the search strategy begins with finding search terms that are both broad enough to include relevant items and narrow enough to exclude irrelevant ones. Both the terms "crime" and "drugs" (or "drug use") are too broad, but a search that combines them (i.e., "crime and drug use") should be specific enough.

ContentSelect Academic Journals

Because studies crime and drug use are reported in scholarly journals in criminal justice, as well as sociology, the search will be conducted in the ContentSelect Academic Journals database for both of these disciplines. To search two or more subject areas, hold down the [Ctrl] key while clicking on each area. This procedure, searching on the phrase "crime and drug use" in both "sociology" and "criminal justice" databases produced 55 articles, including the following 17 titles that seem closely related to the central question of the search:

- STRAINED LIVES AND CRIME: EXAMINING INTRA-INDIVIDUAL VARIATION IN STRAIN AND OFFENDING IN A SAMPLE OF INCARCERATED WOMEN. *Criminology*.
- DIFFERENTIAL PATHWAYS TO VIOLENCE AND SELF-INJURIOUS BEHAVIOR: AFRICAN AMERICAN AND WHITE GIRLS IN THE JUVENILE JUSTICE SYSTEM. *Journal of Research* in *Crime & Delinquency*.
- THE TIMING OF PROPERTY CRIME, VIOLENT CRIME, AND SUBSTANCE USE AMONG JUVENILES. *Journal of Research in* Crime *& Delinquency*.
- GENERAL STRAIN, STREET YOUTH AND CRIME: A TEST OF AGNEW'S REVISED THEORY. *Criminology*.
- "GETTING HIGH AND GETTING BY": DIMENSIONS OF DRUG SELLING BEHAVIORS AMONG AMERICAN MEXICAN GANG

MEMBERS IN SOUTH TEXAS. *Journal of Research in Crime & Delinquency.*

- SELF-CONTROL, SOCIAL CONSEQUENCES, AND CRIMINAL BEHAVIOR: STREET YOUTH AND THE GENERAL THEORY OF CRIME. *Journal of Research in Crime & Delinquency.*
- Arrest Referral in London Police Stations: characteristics of the first year. A key point of intervention for drug users? *Drugs: Education, Prevention & Policy.*
- DEVELOPMENTAL ISSUES IN THE IMPACT OF CHILD MAL-TREATMENT ON LATER DELINQUENCY AND DRUG USE. *Criminology.*
- ILLEGAL ACTS COMMITTED BY ADOLESCENTS UNDER THE INFLUENCE OF ALCOHOL AND DRUGS. *Journal of Research in Crime & Delinquency.*
- SOCIAL PROBLEMS AND PATTERNS OF JUVENILE DELIN-QUENCY IN TRANSITIONAL RUSSIA. *Journal of Research in Crime & Delinquency.*
- THE EFFECTS OF SUBSTANCE USE ON SPECIFIC TYPES OF CRIMINAL OFFENDING IN YOUNG MEN. *Journal of Research in Crime & Delinquency.*
- Violent Behaviors, Violent Victimization, and Doping Agents: A Normal Population Study of Adolescents. *Journal of Interpersonal Violence.*
- STRAINED LIVES AND CRIME: EXAMINING INTRA-INDIVIDUAL VARIATION IN STRAIN AND OFFENDING IN A SAMPLE OF INCARCERATED WOMEN. *Criminology.*
- THE LINKS BETWEEN HEROIN, CRACK COCAINE AND CRIME: Where Does Street Crime Fit In? *British Journal of Criminology.*
- Five-Year Outcomes of Therapeutic Community Treatment of Drug-Involved Offenders After Release From Prison. *Crime & Delinquency.*
- The Impact of Drug Use and Crime Involvement on Health Problems Among Female Drug Offenders. *Prison Journal*
- The Revolving Prison Door for Drug-Involved Offenders: Challenges and Opportunities. *Crime & Delinquency.*

Examining the results of this search of ContentSelect Academic Journals, we see that three periodicals provided many of the articles: *Journal of Research in* Crime *& Delinquency, Crime & Delinquency,* and *Criminology.* Additional online and library searches are therefore likely to find other articles in these periodicals relevant to the research question.

New York Times Archive

The search menu for the *New York Times* Archive permits a search of "all," so the first search specified a search for the phrase "crime and drug use" under "all" subjects. This search produced only one article. The search term was therefore changed slightly, to "crime and drugs," producing 25 articles. Among them were 12 that seem relevant to the research topic. Clicking on the headline will direct your Web browser to the full text of an article:

- As Life Returns to New Orleans, So Does Crime
- Doing Executive Time
- Drugs and Arrests: The Unseen Life of a Motel
- Corruption Hampers Mexican Police in Border Drug War
- Mean Streets in the City of Brotherly Rivalry
- Sex Offenders Received Viagra in New Jersey
- A New Life for a Park And Its Neighborhood
- In New Orleans, Look for the Hidden Crimes
- The Miracle That Wasn't
- Down So Long, It Looks Like Up in Trenton
- Mexican Leader Plans to Broaden Antidrug Enforcement Offices
- Metro Briefing

"Best of the Web" Link Library

The first search, where the discipline of "sociology" was specified, offered both "crime" and "drug abuse" in the alphabetical menu of topics. This database does not permit combining topics, so each one was searched separately. The search under "crime" produced the following Web links. Clicking on the title will transfer your browser to the Web site:

> **National Crime Prevention Council**—The National Crime Prevention Council's online resource center, offering information on crime and prevention.
> **Bureau of Justice Statistics**—The U.S. Department of Justice provides statistics on crime and the justice system.
> **National Incident-Based Reporting System (NIBRS) Implementation Program**—The U.S. Department of Justice's Bureau of Justice Statistics hosts this Web site on the NIBRS, its activities, a state-by-state summary, and links to related sites.
> **Best and Worst Cities for Crime**—This study features the best and worst cities for crime in the US from 331 metro areas. Site maintained by Sperling's BestPlaces, which analyzing data about people and places, and rates them for major publications.

Crime Data—Dr. Thomas O'Connor, North Carolina Wesleyan College, maintains these lecture notes on crime data; includes notes on the best sources to find accurate data and many links for information on crime data and statistics.

NIBRS Impediments—Includes information on the impediments to NIBRS (National Incident-Based Reporting System) participation. Site managed by the National Consortium for Justice Information and Statistics.

Exchange on Crime and Punishment—An exchange between William Bennett and Charles Colson on crime and punishment, sponsored by First Things.

Federal Bureau of Investigation—The FBI's home page, providing access to their "most wanted" list and various crime statistics.

Uniform Crime Reports—The Federal Bureau of Investigation (FBI) hosts this portal with information on its Uniform Crime Reporting (UCR) Program.

National Crime Information Center (NCIC)—Homepage for the FBI's National Crime Information Center (NCIC).

Los Angeles Crimes—The Los Angeles Police Department provides these reports on crime statistics for the City of Los Angeles.

Crime Statistics/Crime Indexes—The U.S. Disaster Center Web site provides access to statistics of crimes compiled by the Federal Bureau of Investigation. View charts on how your state ranks in crime compared to other states during 1960 and 2000.

The search term "drug abuse" produced the following Web links:

National Institute on Drug Abuse—Resource including regularly updated research reports, downloadable therapy manuals for various types of addiction, and useful information on different drugs and their effects on the mind and body.

Drug War Facts—Downloadable research and fact brochures on various aspects of drug use and abuse, including use by women, drug testing, crack babies, methadone, medicinal marijuana use, needle exchange, and race issues. Published by Common Sense for Drug Policy, a nonprofit organization.

Office of National Drug Control Policy—Official site that offers drug prevention and education information for parents and educators, profiles of treatment options, research papers and studies, law enforcement information, and drug facts and figures.

Drug PolicyAlliance—This nonprofit organization offers alternatives to current drug policies, with information about marijuana legalization, a newsletter, and alternative drug policy reforms.

ACDE Home Page—The American Council for Drug Education offers educational information about drug abuse for parents and teachers, as well as a library of sites, research, articles, and signs and symptoms of drug use.

National Center on Addiction and Substance Abuse—Facts about the national and community impact, and costs of substance abuse with specific information about drug use among women, youth, urban residents, and drug-related legislation.

Drug Dependence—Organization of scientists that is devoted to research on substance abuse and addiction. The site features membership information, policy statements on specific substances, and research fact sheets. Maintained by the CPDD.

Partnership for a Drug-Free America—Comprehensive site that includes information about dozens of specific drugs, including what the drug looks like, how it is used, negative effects, and other facts. This site also offers answers to frequently asked questions and support for parents.

National Institute on Alcohol Abuse and Alcoholism—National Institute on Alcohol Abuse and Alcoholism offers a program overview, publications, quick facts, research, and press releases.

Resource Library—Library of facts and information about various drugs and drug abuse issues with links to research resources. Site maintained by the Drug Reform Coordination Network.

Alcohol and Drug Information—A wealth of information on specific drugs and drug abuse with facts and statistics, teaching guides, and research. Site maintained by the NCADI.

Health Services—The Substance Abuse and Mental Health Services Administration offers statistics, research, and facts on various substances and substance abuse issues, as well as treatment advice.

Drug & Crime Facts—The U.S. Department of Justice's Bureau of Justice Statistics hosts this Web site on drug use and crime facts in the U.S.

Relationship Between Addiction to Narcotic Drugs and Crime—United Nations report examines how narcotic drugs and crime are related.

Alcohol Consumption and Increase in Crime in the U.K.— Explore this database of articles on the relationship between alcohol abuse and crime in the United Kingdom.

Although all these Web links are likely to have some information relevant to the crime-drug research question, the single most promising of these Web links appears to be Drug & Crime Facts. According to the statement on the homepage: "This site summarizes U.S. statistics about drug-related crimes, law enforcement, courts, and corrections from Bureau of Justice Statistics (BJS) and non-BJS sources."

Below is a list of possible search topics in sociology, along with key words that could be used as search terms related to each topic:

TOPIC	SEARCH TERMS
Age	Aging, ageism, adolescence, childhood, adulthood, life expectancy, Social Security, safety net
Applied sociology	Market research, social planning
Culture	Cultural lag, ethnocentrism, cultural relativism, subcultures, values, norms
Deviance	Norms, white-collar crime, labeling, differential association, control theory, strain theory, medicalization, drug/alcohol abuse
Economy	Work, globalization, welfare reform, industrialization, multi-national corporations, capitalism, socialism
Education	School, credentialing, cultural transmission, gatekeeping
Environment	Global warming, urbanization, greenhouse emissions, environmental justice, energy sources
Family	Courtship, marriage, co-habitation, descent, patriarchy, child rearing, empty nest, cohabitation, divorce, domestic violence
Formal organizations	Bureaucracy, corporations, rationalization of society, alienation, corporate culture, Milgram, Asch
Politics	Power, authority, government, voting, charismatic authority, democracy, socialism, pluralism
Population	Demography, demographic transition, fertility, mortality, migration, abortion, family planning
Race/ethnicity	Racism, apartheid, caste, segregation, assimilation, multiculturalism, pluralism, discrimination
Religion	Churches, spirituality, fundamentalism, cults
Research methods	Surveys, interviewing, unobtrusive measures, focus groups, research ethics
Sex and Gender	Sexism, glass ceiling, pay equity, patriarchy, feminism, sexual harassment

Social change	Globalization, democratization, invention, discovery, diffusion
Social class	Occupational prestige, wealth, income, educational attainment
Social control	Courts, police, prisons, conformity
Social groups	Gangs, peers, primary groups, secondary groups, small world phenomenon
Social movements	Collective behavior, propaganda, public opinion, terrorism
Social structure	Social class, social status, ascribed status, achieved status,
Social interaction	Stereotypes, personal space, dramaturgy, ethnomethodology, social construction of reality
Socialization	Childhood, resocialization, feral children, peers
Sociological theory	Structural-functionalism, Marxism, symbolic interaction
Stratification	Social class, caste, hierarchy, colonialism
Technology	Computerization, post-industrial society, industrialization
Urbanization	Suburbanization, community, alienation, suburban flight, deindustrialization, gentrification

Useful Journals for Sociology Research

The following list of journals included in the EBSCO database would be useful to find information on the topics listed in the Sample Searches above:

Acta Sociologica
American Anthropologist
American Catholic Sociological
  Review
American Journal of Criminal Justice
American Sociological Review
American Sociologist
Behaviour & Information
  Technology
British Journal of Sociology of
  Education
Canadian Journal of Human
  Sexuality
Canadian Journal of Sociology

Canadian Review of Sociology
  & Anthropology
City Journal of Transnational
  & Crosscultural Studies
Community, Work & Family
Criminologica
Criminology
Cultural Studies
Cultural Trends
Culture Health & Sexuality
Death Studies
Disability, Handicap & Society
Drugs: Education, Prevention
  & Policy

Educational Philosophy & Theory
Environment & Behavior
Ethics & Behavior
Ethics, Place & Environment
Ethnos: Journal of Anthropology
European Societies
Family Therapy—The Journal of
   the California Graduate School
   of Family Psychology
Feminist Issues
Feminist Review
Folklore
Gerontologist
Harvard Gay & Lesbian Review
Health, Risk & Society
Housing, Theory & Society
Human Ecology
Humanist
Identity
Information Society
Information Communication
   & Society
Inquiry
Intercultural Education
International Journal of Social
   Research Methodology
International Review of Sociology
International Social Science Review
Journal of Children & Poverty
Journal of Economic & Social
   Measurement
Journal of Gender Studies
Journal of Health & Social Behavior
Journal of Interpersonal Violence
Journal of Latin American Cultural
   Studies (Travesia)
Journal of Mundane Behavior
Journal of Research in Crime
   & Delinquency

Journal of Research on Adolescence
Journal of Sex Research
Journal of Social Behavior
   & Personality
Journal of Social Forces
Journal of Social Work Practice
Journal of Social, Political
   & Economic Studies
Journal of Sport & Social Issues
Journal of Sport Behavior
Law & Society Review
Mass Communication & Society
Men & Masculinities
Mind, Culture & Activity
Multicultural Perspectives
Personality & Social Psychology
   Review
Population & Development Review
Religion, State & Society
Research on Language & Social
   Interaction
Research on Social Work Practice
Rural Sociology
Sociological Analysis
Science as Culture
Social & Cultural Geography
Social Forces
Social Identities
Social Science & Medicine
Social Science Research
Social Sciences
Social Studies
Social Theory & Practice
Society
Sociological Analysis
Sociological Methods & Research
Sociological Spectrum
Sport, Education & Society
Teaching Sociology

P A R T 4

Online Resources

Internet Sites Useful in Sociology

URLs frequently change or disappear. If you can't find a site, use one of the search engines listed below to look for it by name.

General Useful Sites

American Studies Web

http://www.georgetown.edu/crossroads/asw

Elwell's Glossary of Sociology

http://campus.murraystate.edu/academic/faculty/
frank.elwell/prob3/GLOSSARY/socgloss.htm

Library of Congress

http://www.loc.gov

Maricopa Center for Learning and Instruction

http://www.mcli.dist.maricopa.edu/tl/

SOCNET: Sociology Courses and Curricular Resources

http://www.mcmaster.ca/socscidocs/w3virtsoclib/socnet.htm

World Lecture Hall

http://www.utexas.edu/world/lecture/

Search Engines

AltaVista Search

http://www.altavista.com

Excite Netsearch

http://www.excite.com

Lycos Search

http://www.lycos.com

WebCrawler Search

http://webcrawler.com

Yahoo! Search

http://www.yahoo.com/search.html

General Sociology Sites

American Sociological Association

http://www.asanet.org

BUBL Links: Sociology

http://bublac.uk

Argus Clearinghouse: Social Sciences and Social Issues

http://www.clearinghouse.net/

Electronic Journal of Sociology

http://www.sociology.org/

International Sociological Association

http://www.ucm.es/info/isa

Julian Dierkes' Sociology Links at Princeton

http://www.sociolog.com

Sociological Abstracts Home Page

http://www.csa.com/factsheets/socioabs-set-c.php

Sociological Tour of Cyberspace

http://www.trinity.edu/~mkearl/index.html

Sociology Courses on the Internet

http://www.mcmaster.ca/socscidocs/w3virtsoclib/socnet.htm

Sociology Listservs

http://www.acs.ryerson.ca/soc/listserv.html

Sociology Places to Explore

http://hakatai.mcli.dist.maricopa.edu/smc/ml/sociology.html

Sociology Weblinks at the University of Southern Indiana (USI)

http://www.usi.edu/libarts/SOCIO/weblinks.asp

SocioSite: Sociology in the Netherlands

http://www.sociosite.net/index.php

SOSIG: UK Social Science Information Gateway

http://sosig.esrc.bris.ac.uk

Progressive Sociologists Network

http://www.colorado.edu/sociology/giminez/p5n2

U. C. Berkeley Libraries: Information

http://www.lib.berkeley.edu/find/index.html

U. Colorado's WWW Research Resources for Sociologists

```
http://socsci.colorado.edu/SOC/Research/centers.
html
```

U. Missouri-St. Louis Sociology Links

```
http://www.umsl.edu/~sociolog/resource.htm
```

Western Connecticut State University's Sociology Internet Resources

```
http://www.wcsu.edu/socialsci/socres.html
```

National Technology Transfer Center

```
http://www.nttc.edu/resources/government/
govresources.asp
```

Yahoo!: Sociology

```
http://dir.yahoo.com/Social_Science/Sociology
```

Aging

The AARP Guide to Internet Resources Related to Aging

```
http://www.aarp.org/internetresources/
```

Administration on Aging

```
http://www.aoa.dhhs.gov
```

USC Online Periodicals on Aging

```
http://www.usc.edu/isd/elecresources/subject/
social_Geront.html
```

AOA Homepage

```
http://www.aoa.dhhs.gov/
```

Clifton E. Barber's Internet Information on Aging

```
http://lamar.colostate.edu/~barberhd/
Internetaginglinks.htm
```

U. of Toronto Institute for Life Course and Aging

```
http://www.utoronto.ca/lifecourse
```

Institute for Global Communication's Communities of Activists and Organizations

http://www.igc.org/igc

No Compromise's Activist Links

http://www.nocompromise.org/resources/index.html

Criminology, Deviance, and Criminal Justice

Academy of Criminal Justice Sciences

http://www.acjs.org/

Access to Justice Network (Canadian)

http://www.acjnet.org

American Bar Association

http://www.abanet.org

American Correctional Association

http://www.aca.org/

American Society of Criminology

http://www.asc41.com/

Bureau of Justice Statistics

http://www.ojp.usdoj.gov/bjs

Canadian Centre on Substance Abuse

http://www.ccsa.ca/ccsa

Court TV Online

http://www.courttv.com

The Critical Criminology Division of the American Society of Criminology

http://www.critcrim.org

Drug Reform Coordination Network

http://www.drcnet.org

International Legal Resource Group

http://www.ilrg.com

Justice Information Center

http://www.ncjrs.gov/

National Institute on Drug Abuse (NIDA)

http://www.nida.nih.gov/NIDAHome.html

National Institute of Justice

http://www.ojp.usdoj.gov/nij/

National Center for Victims of Crime

http://www.ncvc.org

PAVNET: Partnerships Against Violence Network

www.pavnet.org

Prevention Online (Prevline)

http://www.health.org

United States Parole Commission

http://www.usdoj.gov/uspc/

Yahoo!: Crime

http://www.yahoo.com/society_and_culture/crime

Juvenile Delinquency

Juvenile Justice WWW Sites

http://www.ncjrs.gov/App/Topics/Topic.aspx?
TopicID=145

Office of Juvenile Justice and Delinquency Prevention

http://ojjdp.ncjrs.gov/

Resources for Working with At Risk Youth

http://iccs.csumb.edu/html/community/riskyouth/index.html

Vision Quest Program for At-Risk Youth

http://www.vq.com/

Culture

Chinese Historical and Cultural Project

http://www.chcp.org

Cultures of the Andes

http://www.andes.org/

Exploring Ancient World Cultures

http://eawc.evansville.edu/index.htm

French Culture

http://gofrance.about.com/?once=true&

The Library of Congress: American Memory

http://rs6.loc.gov

Native American Arts, Humanites and Culture

http://www.tahtonka.com/

NativeWeb: Earth's Indigenous People

www.nativeweb.org

Russian Culture

http://www.auburn.edu/~mitrege/russian-culture/internet-resources.html

University of Colorado Libraries Israel Links

http://ucblibraries.colorado.edu/govpubs/for/israel.htm

U. of Oregon Center for Asian and Pacific Studies

http://darkwing.uoregon.edu/~caps

U. of Virginia: The Multicultural Pavilion

http://www.edchange.org/multicultural

World Culture

http://hometown.aol.com/bowermanb/culture.html

Databanks and Providers

General Social Survey

http://www.icpsr.umich.edu/gss

UCSD Social Sciences Data Collection

http://ssds.ucsd.edu/

U.S. Statistical Abstract

http://www.census.gov/compendia/

Demography, Population, and Urbanization

U.S. Census Bureau Fact Finder

http://www.factfinder.census.gov/home/saff/main.html

Population Reference Bureau

http://www.prb.org/

Center for Demography and Ecology at U. of Wisconsin–Madison

http://www.ssc.wisc.edu/cde/

United Nation's Population Information Network

http://www.un.org/popin/

Ciesin's US Demography

http://www.ciesin.org/datasets/us-demog/
us-demog-home.html

Intentional Communities

http://www.ic.org

Manfred Davidmann on Community

http://www.solbaram.org/indexes/cmmuni.html

National Civic League

http://www.ncl.org/

Pennsylvania State University: Population Research Institute

http://www.pop.psu.edu

Princeton University: Office of Population Research Data Archive

http://opr.princeton.edu/archive

Princeton University: Population Index on the Web

http://popindex.princeton.edu

Rural and Small Town Programme

http://www.mta.ca/rstp

Rural Sociological Society

http://ruralsociology.org

Social Science Research Computing Center's Data Library

http://www.spc.uchicago.edu/DATALIB/
datalib.cgi?

The Urban Institute

http://www.urban.org

U.S. Census Bureau

http://www.census.gov

U.S. Census Bureau: Census State Data Centers

http://www.census.gov/sdc/www

U.S. Dept. of Housing and Urban Development: Neighborhood Networks

http://www.hud.gov/nnw/nnwindex.html

U.S. Gazetteer

http://www.census.gov/geo/www/gazetteer/gazette.html

USA CityLink Home Page

http://usacitylink.com

WWW Virtual Library: Demography & Population Studies

http://demography.anu.edu.au/VirtualLibrary

Economy

ASA Section on Organizations, Occupations, and Work

http://campus.northpark.edu/sociology/oow

Bureau of Labor Statistics

http://www.bls.gov/home.htm

Electronic Policy Network

http://www.movingideas.org/

Institute of Industrial Relations

http://violet.berkeley.edu/~iir

Job Accommodation Network

http://janweb.icdi.wvu.edu

LaborNet

http://www.labornet.org

Legal Information Institute: Employment Discrimination Law Materials

http://www.law.cornell.edu/wex/index.php/Main_Page

Manfred Davidmann on Economics

http://www.solbaram.org/indexes/ecnmcs.html

United Mine Workers of America

http://www.umwa.org/homepage.shtml

The Urban Institute: Work and Income

http://www.urban.org/work/index.cfm

U.S. Dept. of Agriculture: Economic Research Service

http://www.ers.usda.gov

Education

American Association of Community Colleges

http://www.aacc.nche.edu/

ERIC Education Resources Information Center

http://www.eric.ed.gov/

Aspen Institute

http://www.aspeninstitute.org/

EduCause: Transforming Education through Information Technologies

http://www.educause.edu/content.asp?PAGE_ID=720&bhcp=1

The Center for Education Reform

http://edreform.com

Commonwealth of Learning

http://www.col.org

Council of the Great City Schools

http://www.cgcs.org

Education World

http://www.education-world.com/

Global Network Academy

http://www.gnacademy.org

National Education Association (NEA)

http://www.nea.org/

UC-Berkeley Education—Psychology Library

http://www.lib.berkeley.edu/EDP/statistics.html

School District Decision Making Information

http://proximityone.com/plsd.htm

U.S. Department of Education

http://www.ed.gov

U.S. Department of Education: Online Resources

http://www.ed.gov/about/contacts/gen/othersites/index.html

Yahoo!: Education

http://www.yahoo.com/Education

Environment

The British Columbia Ministry of Environment

http://www.gov.bc.ca/wlap

Free U. of Brussels Centre for Economic and Social Studies on the Environment

http://www.ulb.ac.be:80/ceese

Ecology Society of America

http://www.esa.org/

EcoNet

http://www.igc.org/index.html

EcoTrust

http://www.ecotrust.org

EnviroLink

http://www.envirolink.org/

U.S. Government Statistics on the Environment

http://www.fedstats.gov/programs/environ.html

Linkages: Resources for Environment and Development Policy Makers

http://www.iisd.ca/

National Environmental Trust

http://www.environet.org

National Council for Science and the Environment

http://www.cnie.org/nle/

Renewable Energy Policy Project & Center for Renewable Energy and Sustainable Technology (REPP-CREST)

http://www.crest.org

Student Environmental Action Coalition

http://www.seac.org

The Water Environment Federation

http://www.wef.org/

Yahoo!: Environment and Nature Organizations

http://www.yahoo.com/Society_and_Culture/
Environment_and_Nature/Organizations

Yahoo!: Pollution Activist Groups

```
http://www.yahoo.com/Society_and_Culture/
Environment_and_Nature/Pollution/Activist_Groups
```

Ethics

Applied Ethics Resources on WWW

```
http://www.ethics.ubc.ca/resources/
```

Institute for Global Ethics

```
http://www.globalethics.org/
```

HHS Office of Human Research Protections (OHRP)

```
http://www.hhs.gov/ohrp/
```

Family

DHHS Administration for Children and Families

```
http://www.acf.dhhs.gov
```

National Council on Family Relations

```
http://www.ncfr.org/families/relationships.asp
```

ASA Family Section

```
http://www2.asanet.org/sectionfamily/
```

Family Village Library

```
http://www.familyvillage.wisc.edu/library.htm
```

Ring of Single Parents

```
http://c.webring.com/hub?ring=sfvoices
```

University of Amsterdam's Sociosite: Sociology of Family and Children

```
http://www.sociosite.net/topics/familychild.php
```

Gender

Above & Beyond's Gender Resources Newsletters

http://www.abgender.com/news/index.shtml

American Association of University Women

http://www.aauw.org/

Activist and Feminist Resources on the Net

http://polsci.colorado.edu/RES/act.html

Feminist.Com: Resources and Links

http://www.feminist.com/resources/links

The Feminist Majority: Internet Gateway

http://www.feminist.org/

Feminists for Free Expression

http://www.ffeusa.org

Gay and Lesbian Alliance Against Defamation

http://www.glaad.org/

Gender and the Law at the University of Dayton

http://academic.udayton.edu/gender/

Gender and Sexuality Links

http://eserver.org/gender

Gender-Related Electronic Forums

http://www-unix.umbc.edu/~korenman/wmst/forums.
html

Ingersoll Gender Center

http://www.ingersollcenter.org/

National Gay & Lesbian Task Force

http://www.ngltf.org/

National Organization of Women

http://www.now.org/

Voice of the Shuttle: Gender and Sexuality Studies

http://vos.ucsb.edu/browse.asp?id=2711

Women and Gender Studies Links at Louisiana State University (LSU)

http://www.lsu.edu/wgs/links.htm

WomensNet

http://www.voiceofwomen.com/other.html

Women's Studies/Women's Issues Resource Sites

http://www-unix.umbc.edu/~korenman/wmst/links.html

WWWomen! Search Directory for Women Online

http://www.wwwomen.com

Men's Voices Magazine

http://www.menweb.org/

Yahoo!: Men's Movement Organizations

http://dir.yahoo.com/society_and_culture/cultures_and_groups/men/men_s_movement/organizations

Yahoo!: Gender

http://dir.yahoo.com/Society_and_Culture/Gender

Medicine and Health

Aids.org

http://www.aids.org/

American Cancer Society: Cancer Reference Information

http://www.cancer.org/docroot/cri/cri_0.asp

ASH Links to Smoking Related Sites

http://ash.org/otherweb/index.html

Centers for Disease Control & Prevention

http://www.cdc.gov

Department of Health and Human Services

http://www.os.dhhs.gov

HealthLinks

http://healthlinks.washington.edu

Medicine and Health Sources at Bridgewater State University

http://www.bridgew.edu/library/medicine.cfm

Medicine Online: Medical Related Sites

http://www.mol.net

University of Texas' Health and Wellness Sites

http://biotech.icmb.utexas.edu/pages/science/
health.html

World Health Organization

http://www.who.int/en/

Yahoo!: Health

http://dir.yahoo.com/Health

Media

Computer Mediated Communication Magazine Index

http://www.december.com/cmc/mag

Just Think Foundation

http://www.justthink.org/

American Media Association: Mass Media and Culture Resources

http://www.uark.edu/~aca/studies/mediaculture.html

The Media History Project

http://mediahistory.umn.edu

Freedom Forum

http://www.freedomforum.org/

Project Censored: News That Didn't Make the News

http://www.projectcensored.org/

Visionary Media

http://www.visionarymedia.com/

Yahoo!: News and Media

http://dir.yahoo.com/News_and_Media

News Media Online

CNN Digest

http://cnn.com/

Jerusalem Post

http://www.jpost.com/

Mojo Wire (Mother Jones Interactive)

http://www.mojones.com

National Public Radio Online

http://www.npr.org

Newspapers On Line

http://www.onlinenewspapers.com/

NY Times

http://www.nytimes.com/

Public Broadcasting System (PBS) Online

http://www.pbs.org/

Seattle Times

http://seattletimes.nwsource.com/html/home/
index.html

The Times and The Sunday Times

http://www.timesonline.co.uk/global/

USA Today

http://www.usatoday.com/

Politics

African National Congress Home Page

http://www.anc.org.za/

Congressional Quarterly Inc.

http://www.cq.com/

Federal Citizen Information Center

http://pueblo.gsa.gov

C-SPAN

http://www.c-span.org

Moving Ideas: Electronic Policy Network

http://www.movingideas.org/

League of Women Voters

http://www.lwv.org/

National Political Index

http://www.politicalindex.com

The Organization of American States

http://www.oas.org

Political Resources on the Net

http://www.politicalresources.net

Politics1

http://www.politics1.com/

Project Vote Smart

http://www.vote-smart.org

Virtual Tour of the U.S. Government

http://www.virtualfreesites.com/us.government.html

Yahoo!: Politics

http://dir.yahoo.com/Government/Politics

Poverty and Homelessness

HomeAid America: Building Hope and Homes for the Temporarily Homeless

http://www.homeaid.org/home.html

HungerWeb

http://www.nutrition.tufts.edu/academic/
hungerweb/

Institute for Research on Poverty

http://www.irp.wisc.edu/

Homeless People and the Internet

http://www.bmdavidson.tripod.com/

Joint Center for Poverty Research

http://www.jcpr.org/

Michigan Program on Poverty and Social Welfare Policy

http://www.fordschool.umich.edu/research/poverty/

National Center for Children in Poverty

http://www.nccp.org/index.html

National Coalition for the Homeless Directories

http://www.nationalhomeless.org/resources/state/
index.html

National Coalition for the Homeless

http://www.nationalhomeless.org/index.html

National Law Center on Homelessness and Poverty

http://www.nlchp.org/

Resources for Ending Poverty and Hunger

http://www.results.org/website/article.asp?id=19

Century Foundation

http://www.tcf.org/

UMCOR Hunger/Poverty Ministries

http://gbgm-umc.org/umcor/hunger.stm

UN ReliefWeb: Related Sites List

http://www.reliefweb.int/rw/rwc.nsf/doc427?
openform&query=LIB

U.S. Census Bureau: Poverty

http://www.census.gov/hhes/www/poverty/poverty.html

U.S. DHHS: Federal Poverty Guidelines and Measurement

http://aspe.hhs.gov/poverty/index.shtml

Yahoo!: Welfare Reform

http://dir.yahoo.com/Society_and_Culture/
Issues_and_Causes/Poverty/Welfare/Reform

Race and Ethnicity

Race and Ethnicity Collection

http://race.eserver.org/

Cultural Survival

http://209.200.101.189/

European Research Centre on Migration and Ethnic Relations

http://www.ercomer.org

Ethics Updates Page on Race, Multiculturalism and Ethnicity

http://ethics.acusd.edu/applied/race/index.asp

The Final Call: Black Community Issues and Events

http://www.finalcall.com

General Race & Ethnicity Resources—American Studies Web

http://lumen.georgetown.edu/projects/asw/aswsub.
cfm?head1=race%2C%20Ethnicity%2C%20Identity

Legal Information Institute: Civil Rights and Discrimination

http://www.law.cornell.edu/wex/index.php/Civil_
rights

National Civil Rights Museum

http://www.civilrightsmuseum.org

Race and Ethnicity Online

http://www.apsanet.org/~rep/

Trinity Sociology: Race and Ethnicity

http://www.trinity.edu/~mkearl/race.html

Voice of the Shuttle: Minority Studies Page

http://vos.ucsb.edu/browse.asp?id=2721

U. of Utrecht WWW Virtual Library: Migration and Ethnic Relations

http://www.ercomer.org/wwwvl/

Yahoo!: Migration and Ethnic Relations

http://dir.yahoo.com/Social_Science/Migration_
and_Ethnic_Relations

Yahoo!: Race and Racism

http://dir.yahoo.com/Society_and_Culture/Issues_
and_Causes/Race_and_Racism

Religion

American Academy of Religion

http://www.aarweb.org/default.asp

The Center for Reformed Theology and Apologetics

http://www.reformed.org/

Comparative Religion Resources

http://www.lib.washington.edu/subject/
CompReligion/

Cultic Studies

http://www.csj.org/

Fighting the Radical Religious Right (useful links)

http://www.qrd.org/qrd/www/rrr/rrrpage.html

The Search for Truth

http://world.std.com/~awolpert

Index of Religious Links

http://www.religioustolerance.org/toc.htm

Judaism and Jewish Resources

http://shamash.org/trb/judaism.html

Religion Web Sites

http://www.gtu.edu/library/links/index.html

Ontario Consultants on Religious Tolerance

http://www.religioustolerance.org

Religious Movements & Alternative Spirituality,
An Annotated Directory of Internet Resources

http://www.academicinfo.net/nrms.html

Religious Resources on the Net

http://www.religiousresources.org

Religious Studies Electronic Library

http://library.uwaterloo.ca/discipline/religious/

Research Methods

ASA Section on Methods

http://lion.icpsr.umich.edu/methsect

Web Center for Social Research Methods

http://www.socialresearchmethods.net/

The Foundation Center (grants)

http://fdncenter.org

Glossary of Social Science Computing and Social Science
Data Terms

http://odwin.ucsd.edu/glossary

PARnet: The Cornell Participatory Action Research Network

http://www.parnet.org

The Qualitative Report

http://www.nova.edu/ssss/QR/index.html

Resources for Social Researchers

http://www.soc.umn.edu/~edwards/soclinks.htm

Research Methodology Links

http://www2.chass.ncsu.edu/garson/PA765/links.htm

Research Resources for the Social Sciences

http://www.socsciresearch.com

Sociological Research Online

http://www.soc.surrey.ac.uk/socresonline

Statistics

Fedstats: One Stop Shopping for Federal Statistics

http://www.fedstats.gov/

SPSS Inc.

http://www.spss.com

Statistical Resources on the Web: Sociology

http://www.lib.umich.edu/govdocs/stsoc.html

Social Change

CampusActivism.org

http://www.campusactivism.org/

DOE

http://www.energy.gov/index.htm

Good Works: A National Directory of Social Change Organizations

http://goodworksfirst.org/

Internet Resources on Sustainability

http://www.chebucto.ns.ca/Environment/SCN/
CommLink/SCN-netguide.html

Longwave in Socioeconomic Growth and Development

http://www.homestead.com/longwaves/

Peace Brigades International

http://www.igc.apc.org/pbi

Peace Brigades International: Web Links

http://www.igc.apc.org/pbi/links.html

Social Change—A Collection of Relevant Book Chapters

http://ssr1.uchicago.edu//PRELIMS/change.html

Soros Foundation Network for Open Society

http://www.soros.org/

Social Psychology

The British Journal of Social Psychology

http://www.bps.org.uk/publications/journals/bjsp/bjsp_home.cfm

Current Research in Social Psychology

http://www.uiowa.edu/~grpproc/crisp/crisp.html

George Herbert Mead Project

http://spartan.ac.brocku.ca/%7Elward/

Psychology Centre: Social and Cultural Psychology

http://psych.athabascau.ca/html/aupr/social.shtml

Social Psychology Network

http://www.socialpsychology.org/

Social Psychology Resources at Haverford College

http://www.haverford.edu/psych/ble/teaching/links

Society for Personality and Social Psychology

http://www.spsp.org/

A Sociological Social Psychology

http://www.trinity.edu/~mkearl/socpsy.html

SOSIG–World–Social Psychology

http://www.sosig.ac.uk/roads/subject-listing/
World-cat/socpsych.htm

Social Stratification

Albert Benschop's Alphabetical Bibliography on Stratification

http://www2.pfeiffer.edu/~lridener/DSS/socstrat.htm

International Stratification and Mobility File

http://www.sscnet.ucla.edu/issr/da/

Organizational Perspectives on Stratification

http://ssr1.uchicago.edu/PRELIMS/Strat/stmisc1.html

What Is Social Stratification?

http://www.sdsmt.edu/online-courses/is/soc100/
soc_strat.htm

Social Structure and Social Interaction

Alliance for Redesigning Government

http://www.lawguru.com/search/alliancegovt.html

CSIS's Political Economy Archive

http://www.csis.org/simonchair/iipe/

Capitalism.org

http://www.capitalism.org/

Neo-marxism

http://socserv2.mcmaster.ca/soc/courses/soc4s3/
theory/neomarx.htm

A Gallery of Social Structures: Network Visualization

http://www.mpi-fg-koeln.mpg.de/~lk/netvis.html

Max Planck Institute for the Study of Societies

http://www.mpi-fg-koeln.mpg.de

WSN: The World-Systems Conferencing Electronic Network

http://wsarch.ucr.edu/

Sociological Theory

"An Outline of the Social System"

http://ssr1.uchicago.edu/PRELIMS/Theory/parsons.html

ASA Section on Marxist Sociology

http://www.colorado.edu/Sociology/gimenez/section/

Association for Humanist Sociology

http://www.humanistsoc.org

Critical Theory-Driven Inquiry

http://www.uchicago.edu/research/jnl-crit-inq/

CTHEORY

http://www.pactac.net/pactacweb/web-content/
ctheoryindex.html

The Marx/Engels Internet Archive

http://csf.Colorado.edu/psn/marx

Marx and Engels' Writings

http://marx.eserver.org/

Norbert Elias and Process Sociology

http://www.usyd.edu.au/su/social/elias/elias.html

Postmodern Culture

```
http://jefferson.village.virginia.edu/pmc/
contents.all.html
```

Postmodern Thought Links at the University of Colorado, Denver

```
http://carbon.cudenver.edu/~mryder/itc_data/
postmodern.html
```

Society for the Study of Symbolic Interaction

```
http://sun.soci.niu.edu/~sssi
```

Sociology Links from Patrick Macartney

```
http://www.angelfire.com/ma/Socialworld/
Sociology.html
```

Spoon Collective for Discussion of Philosophical Issues

```
http://www.spooncollective.org/
```

Tocqueville's Democracy in America

```
http://xroads.virginia.edu/~HYPER/DETOC/home.html
```

The Works of John Locke

```
http://libertyonline.hypermall.com/Locke/Default.
htm
```

Technology and Computers

Alliance for Public Technology

```
http://apt.org/index.html
```

Association for Computing Machinery

```
http://www.acm.org/
```

Association for Progressive Communications

```
http://www.apc.org
```

The Center for Democracy and Technology

http://www.cdt.org/

Computer Professionals for Social Responsibility

http://www.cpsr.org/

CTHEORY: Journal of Theory, Technology and Culture

http://www.ctheory.net/home.aspx

Scientists for Global Responsibility

http://www.sgr.org.uk/

Society for the Social Studies of Science

http://www.nae.edu/nae/techlithome.nsf/weblinks/
KGRG-58CRPC?OpenDocument

Street-Level Youth Media: Communications Technology for Youth

http://streetlevel.iit.edu/

Violence and Abuse

BC Institute Against Family Violence

http://www.bcifv.org/

ConflictNet: Conflict Resolution Resources

http://www.jca.apc.org/~y-okada/igc/conflictnet/

Domestic Violence Notepad

http://www.womenlawyers.com/domestic.htm

SAFE: Stop Abuse for Everyone

http://www.safe4all.org/info

Links on Violence and Abuse, Q Web Sweden

http://www.qweb.kvinnoforum.se/

MINCAVA: Minnesota Center Against Violence and Abuse

`http://www.mincava.umn.edu`

National Network for Child Care

`http://www.nncc.org/`

National Center on Child Fatality Review

`http://ican-ncfr.org/`

Nonviolence International

`http://www.nonviolenceinternational.net/`

SafetyNet Domestic Violence Resources

`http://home.cybergrrl.com/dv/`

Yahoo!: Domestic Violence Organizations

`http://www.yahoo.com/Society_and_Culture/Crime/`
`Types_of_Crime/Domestic_Violence/Organizations`

Other Online Resources

Allyn & Bacon Social Problems Supersite

`http://www.ablongman.com/socprobs`
The Social Problems Supersite is organized around 14 core social problems topics. The *Where Do You Stand?* Feature offers a series of survey questions designed to prepare students for the various issues within each social problem area. Other features include an online glossary, interactive study guide (with multiple choice, true/false, fill-in-the-blank, and essay questions), internet resources, message board, and critical thinking questions.

Flash Review Series for Introduction to Sociology

`http://www.flashreview.com`
This is the companion Web site to the Flash Review for Introduction to Sociology, a new kind of study guide that features interactive quizzes, career advice, sample tests, and study aides. You can find a copy of the study guide at your local bookseller.

NOTES

NOTES

NOTES

NOTES

NOTES

NOTES

NOTES

NOTES

NOTES

NOTES

NOTES

NOTES